SARA MAKES A PRAYER

Dalia Ramzi Mohammad

Editor: Noor Hammoud
Copyright © 2019 by Dalia Ramzi Mohammad

Sara rested her head on her pillow. Every night before she went to sleep she made a duaa to Allah. Tonight she prayed, "Oh Allah, thank you for such a nice day. Please give me my favorite breakfast in the morning." She then closed her eyes and went to sleep.

The next morning she woke up to the smell of her favorite breakfast: pancakes! She ran downstairs and gobbled them up. She was ready to start her day.

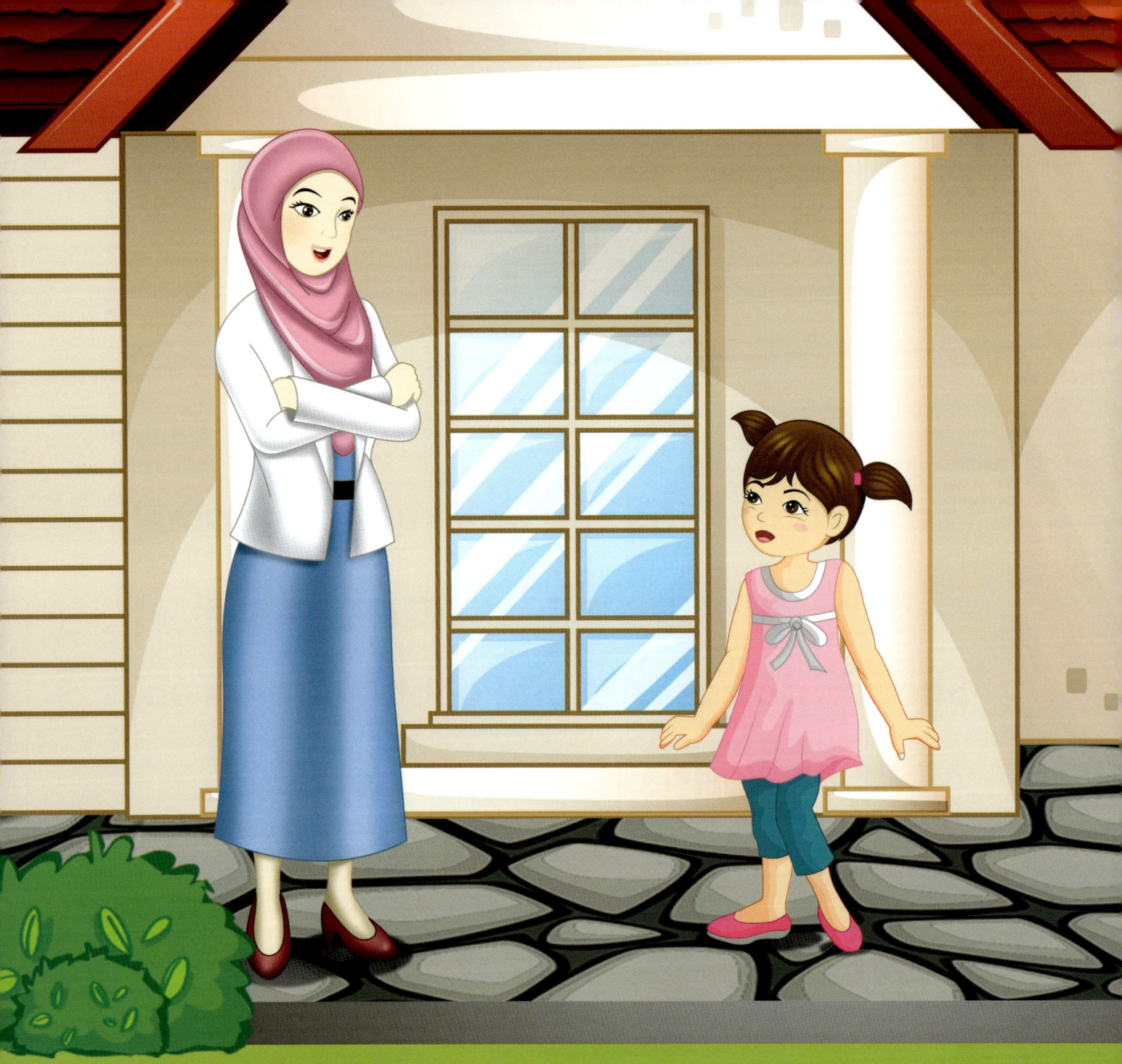

That night she prayed,
"Oh Allah, please give me a new toy."
She woke up the next morning
and searched everywhere.
She could not find any new toy.
She even asked her mom,
but there was nothing.

Sara was very sad.

"How could that be?" she wondered.

"How can Allah not answer my prayer?"

She moped around the house

and then sat in her room.

She was disappointed.

"Sara, what's wrong?" her mom asked. "Mama, I don't understand why Allah did not answer my prayer," Sara replied. "Allah always answers our prayers. Sometimes He gives us exactly what we ask for and sometimes He gives us something different or even better. He always does what is best for us. You have to keep hope in Allah," her mom explained.

The next day, while Sara was playing outside, her neighbor came up to her.
"Sara, do you want one of my kittens?" she asked.
Sara could not believe it!
She always dreamed of having a kitten.
She ran inside to ask her mom.
Her mom said yes! Sara was so excited.

Sara hugged her new kitten
and took it up to her room.
She said, "Thank you Allah
for answering my prayer.
You gave me even better
than what I asked for."
She kissed the kitten and whispered to it,
"I'm going to name you Hope."

Dedicated to my hearts:

Moumen, Layla, Omar & Lena.

Sincere gratitude to my supportive father,

Ramzi Mohammad. I love you Baba.